Corfu

COLLINS

Glasgow & London

First published 1990
Copyright © William Collins Sons & Company Limited
Published by William Collins Sons & Company Limited
Printed in Hong Kong
ISBN 0 00 435775-2

HOW TO USE THIS BOOK

Your Collins Traveller Guide will help you find your way around your chosen destination quickly and easily. It is colour-coded for easy reference:

The blue-coded 'topic' section answers the question 'I would like to see or do something; where do I go and what do I see when I get there?' A simple, clear layout provides an alphabetical list of activities and events, offers you a selection of each, tells you how to get there, what it will cost, when it is open and what to expect. Each topic in the list has its own simplified map, showing the position of each item and the nearest landmark or transport access, for instant orientation. Whether your interest is Architecture or Food you can find all the information you need quickly and simply. Where major resorts within an area require in-depth treatment, they follow the main topics section in alphabetical order.

The red-coded section is a lively and informative gazetteer. In one alphabetical list you can find essential facts about the main places and cultural items - 'What is La Bastille?', 'Who was Michelangelo?' - as well as practical and invaluable travel information. It covers everything you need to know to help you enjoy yourself and get the most out of your time away, from Accommodation through Babysitters, Car Hire, Food, Health, Money, Newspapers, Taxis and Telephones to Zoos.

Cross-references: Type in small capitals - **CHURCHES** - tells you that more information on an item is available within the topic on churches. A-Z in bold - **A-Z** - tells you that more information is available on an item within the gazetteer. Simply look under the appropriate heading. A name in bold - **Holy Cathedral** - also tells you that more information on an item is available in the gazetteer under that particular heading.

Packed full of information and easy to use - you'll always know where you are with your Collins Traveller Guide!

Photographs by **Neil Wilson**

Corfu is, in the late 20thC, as beguiling as ever. The crescent-shaped island can still bewitch - as it did Homer and Shakespeare - despite all the attendant, sometimes overbearing, interest that its fine features attract. In *The Tempest* (Act II, Scene 1) Shakespeare evoked its 'subtle, tender and delicate temperance'. 'How lush and lusty the grass looks! how green!'. If you climb into a pine wood in the island's interior it might just be possible to imagine things haven't changed much since. Of course, they have changed dramatically. The pub, taverna and disco culture along the bustling east coast is beloved by the 'lusty' British, and the resorts of Benitses and Kassiopi vibrate to a young, pop beat. This Ionian island, about 96 kilometres by 40, attracts young tourists and is visited by more British holiday-makers than any other Greek island. It has a strangely green look; its verdant slopes are a dramatic contrast to the sparse vegetation of bustling Mykonos or Santorini in the Dodecanese away to the south east. You can find slopes carpeted in wild flowers and hills laden with cypress and citrus and lemon groves. The predominant tree is the olive, on which the island's Venetian conquerors once based a thriving economy. Today the Corfiots make money out of the tourists who come each summer to worship the sun. Despite the rich overlay of cultures which once fought and squabbled over the island, it retains no major architectural wonders, but many legacies of past rulers. Kerkyra, the name given to the island by the Dorians of Corinth, the first settlers, has had an astonishingly turbulent passage to the 20thC. Although it may be hard to imagine today, the island was once an important, rich land at the centre of civilization. In the 14thC the Venetians took over the island. They fought bitterly with the Turks in the 16thC and finally lost possession of Corfu two centuries later to Napoleon and the French. By 1815 it was a free state with British protection, following the Treaty of Paris. Later in the same century it was restored to the Greeks, and more recently it was bombed by the Italians in 1923 and by the Gemans in 1940. Corfu's affair with the tourist is a relatively recent phenomenon - and, some believe, an ill-fated one.

But it has two jewels which have not been drastically altered by the invading Euro-tourists. The most celebrated is Paleokastritsa, the real beauty spot on Corfu. Lawrence Durrell, a great fan of the island (his book *Prospero's Cell* is about Corfu), once noted that, despite recent developments, Paleokastritsa remained 'a dream place'. It is one of those magical Greek places for sitting, sipping cocktails and watching a giant sun sink into the sea. The sky will change colour a hundred times before the last cocktail has been downed, and the last picture snapped. There are a string of beautiful pebble and sand coves along the coast, nestling beneath steep, rocky cliffs on which cypress and olives stubbornly cling. Choose this resort on Corfu and you will have little reason to be disappointed.

Then there is Corfu Town itself, a picturesque, cosmopolitan city which can be educational, chic and laid-back all in the space of a few attractive cobbled streets. Sit in a street café in Theotoki Square, surrounded by foreign babble and baubles, and watch the world pass by on the back of every form of two-wheeled transport imaginable. Families of four can get by on one scooter. Traffic in Corfu Town is all gesticulation, braking and honking of horns; motorbikes bearing dark, tousle-haired guys with long-legged girls hanging on behind them. The city is at its most attractive around *Paleo Frourio*, the Old Fort, and along the esplanade which climbs past Neoclassical buildings from the quayside and the ferry terminals towards the old part of the city. Corfu boasts attractive parks, good restaurants, cafés and boutiques and has a cross-European atmosphere which you are unlikely to find in other parts of the island. Unless you have to be on a beach, it's well-worth basing your visit in Corfu Town and using a hired car for the rest of the island. Wherever you go you should go to Corfu knowing that you will not find Shakespeare's isle, or even Durrell's isle, but an island which has been transformed by tourism and sometimes insensitive development. However, you can be sure its climate and its lively image will keep on attracting visitors. And, with a little bit of effort, you may find your own ideal somewhere on Kerkyra and discover why the island has been fought over quite so often.

Bill McDowall

East/North coast

DASSIA 13 km north of Corfu Town.
Bus no. 7 from San Rocco Square.
Wide bay, bordered by olive trees. Watersports at camp sites and hotels.

IPSOS/PYRGI 16 km north of Corfu Town.
Kassiopi bus from New Fortress Square.
Long, narrow stretch of beach. Camp sites, hotels and lively nightlife.

BARBATI 18 km north of Corfu Town.
Kassiopi bus from New Fortress Square.
Lovely long pebble beach screened from the road by olive groves. Quiet.

NISSAKI 23 km north of Corfu Town.
Kassiopi bus from New Fortress Square.
Delightful small creek with exceptionally clear blue water. Beach hotel.

KALAMI 30 km north of Corfu Town.
Kassiopi bus from New Fortress Square.
Beautiful small bay with narrow stony beach, once home to Lawrence Durrell. Readers of Prospero's Cell *will recognize the area. Taverna.*

KASSIOPI 36 km north of Corfu Town.
Bus from New Fortress Square.
Historic port and busy resort with a shingle beach. See EXCURSION 1, **A-Z**.

RODA 38 km north west of Corfu Town.
Bus from New Fortress Square.
Fishing village above a crescent-shaped sandy beach. See EXCURSION 1.

ASTRAKERI 36 km north of Corfu Town.
Best reached by car.
Quiet beach reached through pleasant inland village of Karusades.

SIDARI 35 km north west of Corfu Town.
Bus from New Fortress Square.
Long, sandy beach with many small coves carved into the sandstone cliffs.

Sidari

Roda

Kassiopi

Mt. Pantocrator

Spartylas

Nissaki

Barbati

Pyrgi

Ipsos

Dassia

Gouvia

PALEO-
KASTRITSA

Corfu

AGIOU
GEORGIOU
BAY

Pelekas

ERMONES

MYRTIOTISSA

Perama

GLYFADA

Sinarades

Benitses

AGIOS
GORDIOS

Moraitika

MESSONGHI

LAKE
KORISSION

Lefkimmi

AGIOS
GEORGIOS

KAVOS

West Coast

AGIOU GEORGIOU BAY 35 km north west of Corfu Town.
Via Troumpeta and Pagi by road; from Paleokastritsa by boat.
Wide, sandy, relatively isolated beach becoming increasingly popular.

PALEOKASTRITSA 26 km west of Corfu Town.
Bus from New Fortress Square.
Picturesque resort; beautiful scenery and beaches. See EXCURSION 2, **A-Z**.

ERMONES 15 km west of Corfu Town.
Vatos-Glyfada bus from New Fortress Square.
Sandy bay now extensively developed as a resort. See EXCURSION 2.

MYRTIOTISSA 16 km west of Corfu Town.
Walk from Ermones/Peleka; boat from Ermones, Glyfada, Paleokastritsa.
Sheer cliffs, sandy beach, crystal water. Unofficial nudist beach.

GLYFADA 17 km west of Corfu Town.
Below Peleka village, bus from New Fortress Square.
Beautiful sandy beach suitable for everyone. Facilities at beach hotel.

AGIOS GORDIOS 26 km south west of Corfu Town.
Ag. Gordios-Sinarades bus from New Fortress Square.
Glorious sands framed by vineyards and sheer cliffs. See EXCURSION 2.

AGIOS GEORGIOS-LAKE KORISSION 28 km south west of
Corfu. Kavos-Lefkimmi bus from New Fortress Sq.; car - off Lefkimmi
road at Linia to Korission; Ag. Georgios turn off two km after Linia.
Windswept, golden dunes, no shade or fresh water. Facilities - Ag. Georgios.

KAVOS 47 km south of Corfu Town.
Kavos-Lefkimmi bus from New Fortress Square.
Busy, rather crowded resort with long beach and clear, shallow water.

MESSONGHI 23 km south of Corfu Town.
Messonghi bus from New Fortress Square; car - off Lefkimmi road.
Clean sand, shallow water but narrow and crowded. See EXCURSION 2.

EXCLUSIVE 39 Voulgareos St., Corfu Town.
• 0900-1500, 1700-2200 Mon.-Sat.
Handwoven goat hair and wool rugs. Delivery service all over the world. Also Greek art, pottery, etc.

CORFU LEATHER WORKSHOP 57 Nik. Theotoki St., Corfu Town.
• 0800-2200 Mon.-Sat.
High-quality belts and bags made exclusively for this shop.

KUVDIA 52 Guilford St., Corfu Town.
• 0900-2100 daily.
Contemporary ceramics, earrings and batik silk scarves.

ALKIS Lakones.
• Daily.
Small roadside shop with varied display of olive wood bowls and pots, all handmade on the premises.

ALEKA'S LACE HOUSE Kassiopi (far right end of harbour).
• 0830-2300 Mon.-Sat.
A fine assortment of tablecloths, bedspreads, pillowcases, aprons, etc. Visited by Princess Margaret once every year!

THE CRAFTHOUSE 22 Kapodistriou, Corfu Town.
• 0900-2300 Mon.-Sat., 0900-1430 Sun.
Very attractive handmade brass and copperware.

DANILIA VILLAGE 9 km north west of Corfu Town.
• 1000-1300, 1800-2200.
*A collection of shops selling silver jewellery and olive wood goods (both made on the premises) plus leather bags, tapestry wall-hangings and cushion covers, and Corfiot ceramics, all very reasonably priced. See **A-Z**.*

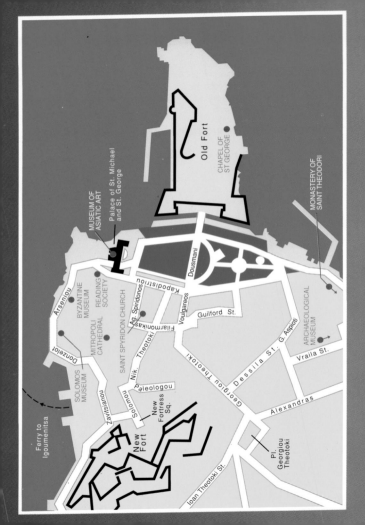

Old Fort

CHAPEL OF
ST GEORGE

MUSEUM OF
ASIATIC ART

Palace of St. Michael
and St. George

MONASTERY OF
SAINT THEODORI

Dousmani

Kapodistrion

Arseniou

BYZANTINE
MUSEUM

READING
SOCIETY

Ag. Spiridonos

Philarmonikas

Voulgareos

Guilford St.

ARCHAEOLOGICAL
MUSEUM

Donzeloti

MITROPOLI
CATHEDRAL

SAINT SPYRIDON CHURCH

Nik. Theotoki

Georgiou Theotoki

Dessila St. G. Aspioti

Vraila St.

Ferry to
Igoumenitsa

SOLOMOS
MUSEUM

Zavitsianou

Solomou

Paleologou

New
Fortress
Sq.

Alexandras

New
Fort

Ioan Theotoki St.

Pl.
Georgiou
Theotoki

SAINT SPYRIDON CHURCH Old Town.
Houses relics of the Patron Saint of the island. See **Events, St Spyridon**.

MITROPOLI CATHEDRAL Mitropoleos St.
• 0800-1330, 1630-2030. Near Old Port where Igoumenitsa boats moor.
The silver reliquary containing remains of St Theodora is opened annually.

CHAPEL OF ST GEORGE The Old Fort.
• 0800-1900 (Old Fort).
Originally an Anglican garrison chapel, restored after Second World War.

MONASTERY OF SAINT THEODORI Old Corfu.
• 0800-1330, 1600-1930. Road marked 'Stratia' to right of Monrepos.
Vestiges of an Archaic altar and a Temple of Artemis can be seen.

ARCHAEOLOGICAL MUSEUM 1 Vraila St.
• 0800-1500 Tues.-Sun. Along Demokratias. • 200 Drs.
Corfu's history told through artefacts from local excavations. See **A-Z.**

MUSEUM OF ASIATIC ART Palace of St Michael and St-George
(Royal Palace).
• 0845-1500 Tues.-Sat., 0930-1430 Sun., hols. • 400 Drs.
Outstanding collection of Sino-Japanese art housed in the Palace. See **A-Z.**

BYZANTINE MUSEUM 3 Parados Arseniou St.
• 0845-1500 Mon., Wed., Thurs., Fri., Sat., 0930-1430 Sun. In the old
Antivouniotissa Church.
Collection of 13th-17thC icons.

SOLOMOS MUSEUM 41 Arseniou St.
• 1700-2000 Mon., Wed., Thurs., Fri. • 50 Drs.
Museum dedicated to Dyonisis Solomos, Greece's national poet.

READING SOCIETY 120 Capodistrias St.
• 0900-1400 daily.
Collection of books, manuscripts and prints on Ionian history and culture.

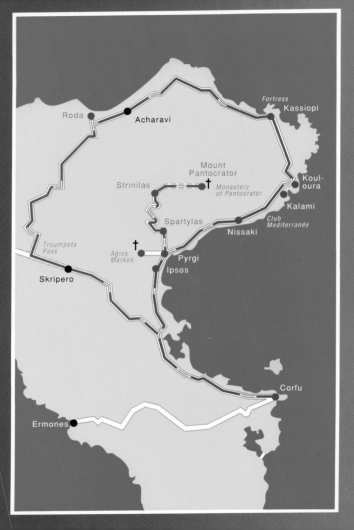

North

A one-day trip north from Corfu Town through various resorts along the coast and inland to Mount Pantocrator, the highest peak on the island.

Leave Corfu Town heading north.

15 km - Ipsos. A fishing village in the heart of this highly developed, tourist-orientated stretch of coast (see **BEACHES 1**). Visit the local church which contains 11thC frescoes.

16 km - Pyrgi. Here you should visit Agios Pantocrator, a 16thC church with interesting details, and also **Agios Markos** (2 km west of Pyrgi) a small village with a pretty 11thC church. There are spectacular views from the courtyard outside (see **SIGHTSEEING 3**).

Fork left after Pyrgi towards Spartylas (7 km), then turn off right about 1 km after Spartylas to Strinilas (29 km). Two hours' walk from here is the summit of Mount Pantocrator (906 m) crowned by a l4thC monastery which commands wonderful views over the whole of the island (see **SIGHTSEEING 3, WALK 1**). Return to Pyrgi and then turn left and continue along the coast road.

22 km - Nissaki. A small beach resort with holiday apartments.

28 km - Kalami and **Kouloura** (2 km north). A short detour from the main road will bring you to either of these seaside villages. Lawrence Durrell's 'White House', now part-taverna, is at Kalami. See **BEACHES 1**.

36 km - Kassiopi (see **A-Z**). Founded in 300 BC by Pyrrhus of Epirus. The rocky beach is overlooked by ruins of a 13thC fortress. See **SIGHTSEEING 3**.

48 km - Roda. A popular fishing village with rugged scenery and sandy beaches (see **BEACHES 1**). From Roda take the southern road which passes through the Troumpeta Pass with glimpses of the mountainous northern region. Turn left just after the pass to return to Corfu (20 km) passing through countryside typical of the island.

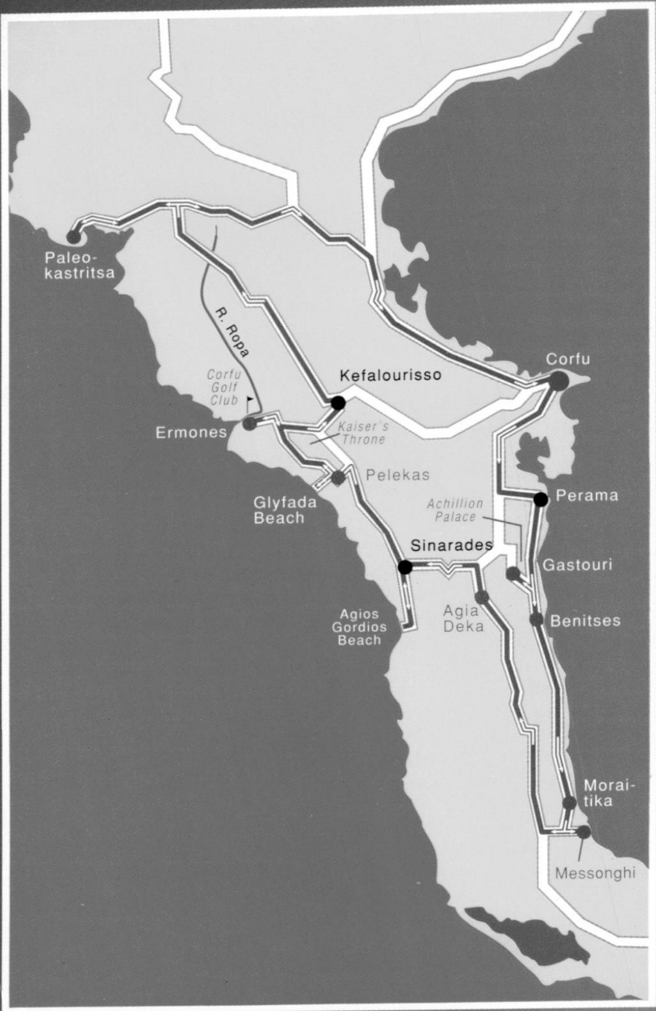

Paleo-
kastritsa

R. Ropa

Corfu
Golf
Club

Kefalourisso

Corfu

Ermones

Kaiser's
Throne

Pelekas

Perama

Glyfada
Beach

Achillion
Palace

Sinarades

Gastouri

Agios
Gordios
Beach

Agia
Deka

Benitses

Morai-
tika

Messonghi

Paleokastritsa

A one or two-day excursion visiting some of the island's popular beaches and resorts, including Paleokastritsa, Corfu's most attractive tourist spot.

Take the Perama road out of Corfu Town towards Benitses.

9 km - Gastouri. Visit Achillion's Palace (see **SIGHTSEEING 3, A-Z**).

12.5 km - Benitses. A fishing village and popular tourist spot, with a pebble beach and some Roman remains. See **SIGHTSEEING 3**.

22 km - Messonghi. Drive past the village of Moraitika, which has a fine, sandy beach, and where the main road bends sharply to the right take the narrow road to the left. The road is bordered by beautiful olive trees, some 500 years old, and leads to a clean, shallow beach which is ideal for children. See **BEACHES 2**.

Rejoin the main road and turn right after about 1 km and head north towards Agia Deka. The narrow, winding road passes through wonderful scenery - delightful mountainside villages and lush valleys planted with olive groves. Rejoin the main road and turn left.

45 km - Agios Gordios Beach. One of the most beautiful on the island, with sheer cliffs and fascinating rock formations (see **BEACHES 2**). Rejoin the main road from the beach, then drive north through Sinarades.

56 km - Pelekas. There are wonderful views from this hilltop village - a favourite of Wilhelm II who contemplated the sunsets from a spot now known as the 'Kaiser's Throne'. Turn left from Pelekas.

60 km - Glyfada Beach. A wide, sandy beach bordered by dunes and offering good facilities and which is usually busier than the beach at Pelekas (see **BEACHES 2**). Leave Glyfada and turn left before reaching Pelekas.

65 km - Ermones. A quiet beach (see **BEACHES 2**) at the estuary of the River Ropa amid wild landscape where Odysseus is supposed to have met Nausicaa. The island's only golf course is nearby. Rejoin the road and turn left after 2 km and then left again at Kefalourisso (Corfu Town is to the right).

80 km - Paleokastritsa. This is the most attractive beach resort on the island with its Byzantine monastery perched on the wooded hillside. See **SIGHTSEEING 3, A-Z**.

Take the direct route back to Corfu Town (26 km).

Mainland

A two-day excursion to the mainland visiting sites of religious and his-
torical interest, including Classical ruins, early Christian churches and a
magnificent cave. An overnight stay at Meteora is necessary before the
return journey.

From Corfu Town there are 12 ferries daily to Igoumenitsa on the mainland. The crossing takes approximately two hours and costs 3250 Drs
for a car and two passengers one-way.

From Igoumenitsa take the road east towards Ioannina.

80 km - Ioannina. An ancient Balkan city founded by Emperor Justin in
7thC AD on the shores of Lake Pamvotis. On an island in the lake are
several rather curious monasteries with restored frescoes. Leave
Ioannina heading south for Arta and then turn right for Dodone.

101 km - Dodone. A religious centre dating from 1900 BC, with a
beautiful restored amphitheatre, the site for a festival of classical drama
held the first week in August (0730-1930 Mon.-Sat., 0900-1800 Sun.,
hols; 200 Drs). Return to Ioannina and head east for Metsovo. Just
beyond Ioannina is **Perama Cave**, a spectacular chamber 2 km long
and 10 m high, filled with spectacular stalagmite and stalactite formations with wonderful names such as 'A Dozen Hanging Breasts' or 'Pigs
Coming Down the Hill'! (0800-2000; 300 Drs). Return to the main road
and continue east.

208 km - Metsovo. This mountainside community is a genuine example of the traditional Vlahi culture, whose people speak an Italian
dialect and are possibly descendants of a group trained by the Romans
to guard the Egnatia Highway. Continue east then turn left off the main
road at the village of Kalambaka, drive through Kastraki (2 km) and
follow the signs for Meteora.

296 km - Meteora. Out of the original 24 monasteries perched on top
of strange pillars of rock, only five are still in use. The pinnacles were
first inhabited in the 11thC and became an ideal refuge for Christians
during the invasions of the 12thC. Today these fascinating buildings can
be reached by steps from below and above the road, and the area is a
popular tourist attraction.

Spend the night in one of the local hotels or bed and breakfast establishments before the return journey.

PAXI

From Corfu Town: • Boat leaves 1430 Mon.-Tues., Thurs.-Fri. (3 hr);
return next day. From Kavos: • Boat leaves 0930 Mon.-Tues., Fri.-Sat.
Tiny, fertile island set in lovely clear waters. Spectacular sea caves. See **A-Z.**

ANDIPAXI

From Gaios (Paxi): • Boat leaves 0900-1100; back 1430-1900 (40 min).
Island off the coast of Paxi. Sandy beaches. No accommodation. See **Paxi.**

LEFKADA

• Bus Athens-Patra (4 buses per day, 7 hr) then ferry.
• Boat links from Ithaca (3 hr 30 min) and Kephalonia (4 hr 30 min)
twice a week.
Separated from mainland by a 25 m canal. Good beaches. See **A-Z**.

KEPHALONIA

• To Sami from:	Patra (mainland) - 2 boats per day (4 hr).
	Ithaca - 1 boat per day (l hr 30 min).
	Paxi - 1 boat per week (4 hr).
• To Fiscardo from:	Vassiliki (Lefkada) - 2 boats per day (3 hr).
	Vathi (Ithaca) - 2 boats per day (1 hr).

• Boat links with mainland (Astakos, Mitikas) and Nidri (Lefkada) once a
week during July-Aug. Also ferries from Brindisi, Corfu, Igoumenitsa.
• Air: Olympic Airways from Athens-Argostolion (45 min).
Largest of the Ionian islands. Still unspoiled by the tourist trade. See **A-Z.**

ITHACA

• Lefkada-Frikes 0900 daily (4 hr). Fiscardo (Kephalonia)-Frikes (1 hr).
• Patra (mainland)-Vathi daily (6 hr). Same ferry: Sami (Kephalonia)-
Vathi (1 hr 15 min). • Astakos (mainland)-Vathi daily (2 hr).
Small, rocky island with unspoiled scenery, and lovely beaches. See **A-Z**.

ZAKINTHOS

• From Killini (mainland) 6 ferries daily (1 hr 15 min). • Argostolion
(Kephalonia) 1200 Sun. (3 hr). • Olympic Airways from Athens daily.
Beautiful, wild and mountainous island. Limited accommodation. See **A-Z.**

Sidari   Roda   Kassiopi

Mt.
Pantocrator

Spartylas   Nissaki
ALBATROS   Barbati
       Pyrgi
    Ipsos
Dassia
    BREEZEE

Paleo-
kastritsa

Gouvia   ADONIS DISCO CLUB
DANILIA VILLAGE   LA BOOM
         APOCALYPSIS

Agiou
Georgiou
Bay

Pelekas   Corfu

Ermones   MAI THAI DISCO

Myrtiotissa   Perama
Glyfada

Sinarades   BABYLON
          DISCO   Benitses

Agios
Gordios

              Moraitika
              Messonghi

Lake
Korission

       Agios   Lefkimmi
       Georgios

                Kavos

APOCALYPSIS Ethnikis Antistasis.
• 2230-0300. Ipsos-Pyrgi bus from New Fortress Square. • 1000 Drs.
Up-to-the-minute music at this disco set in stylish surroundings.

LA BOOM Ethnikis Antistasis.
• 2230-0300. Ipsos-Pyrgi bus from New Fortress Square. • 1000 Drs.
An up-market disco housed in converted stables and surrounded by pleasant gardens.

BREEZEE Dassia.
• 2230-0300. Bus no. 7 from San Rocco Square. • Free.
An out-of-town disco very popular with British tourists.

ALBATROS Pyrgi.
• 2200-0300. Ipsos-Pyrgi bus from New Fortress Square. • Free.
Another holiday resort disco which is popular with tourists.

DANILIA VILLAGE
• 2030-2400 Mon.-Sat.
A reconstruction of a typical Corfiot village. During the day you can visit the shops here and at night there is a Greek floorshow. See BEST BUYS, **A-Z.**

MAI THAI DISCO Kanoni.
• 2100-0300. Bus no. 2 (Mandouki-Kanoni) half-hourly 0630-2300.
An English disc jockey plays mostly English disco music with a 60s night on Sundays. The Garden Pub serves food in the evenings.

ADONIS DISCO CLUB Gouvia.
• 2200-0300 (0400 Sat.). Bus no. 7 (Kontokali-Gouvia-Dassia) from San Rocco Square. • Free.
Set in the heart of Gouvia village, this popular disco plays a varied selection of music.

BABYLON DISCO Benitses.
• 2230-0300. Bus no. 6 (Perama-Benitses) from San Rocco Sq. • Free.
A popular disco near the harbour playing a variety of music.

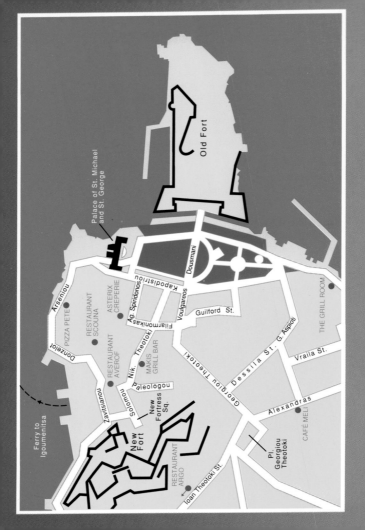

Corfu Town

ASTERIX CREPERIE 40 Sof. Dousmani St.
• 1100-1430, 2000-2300 daily.
Enjoy delicious sweet or savoury pancakes from this French crèperie.

PIZZA PETE Arseniou.
• 1000-0100 daily.
As the name implies, pizzas with a vast range of toppings.

RESTAURANT AVEROF Corner of Odhos Alipiou and
Prossalendou.
• 1100-2400 daily.
Traditional Greek fare at very reasonable prices.

RESTAURANT SCOUNA Mitropoleos St.
• 0800-0100 daily.
*Traditional Greek food in a pleasant setting with views up to the cathedral
and down to the main port.*

RESTAURANT ARGO Ethnikis Antistasis, New Port.
• 1900-0100 daily.
*Fresh lobster and fish are available daily in this expensive but high-quality
restaurant. The service is also good.*

THE GRILL ROOM Corfu Palace Hotel.
• 2000-2300 daily.
*Expensive. A wide range of French dishes is available from the à la carte
menu.*

CAFÉ MELI 30 Alexandras St.
• 1000-1400, 1730-2300 daily.
*Really a pastry shop (street café) but also has a restaurant with a small but
very good menu. Delicious pastries and great service.*

MAKIS GRILL BAR Odhos Alipiou and Prossandelou.
• All day, every day.
Simple Greek food cooked over charcoal. Very good value.

Island

PIEROTTO (top of the steps from Kanoni causeway).
• 1300-2400 daily. Bus no. 6 hourly from San Rocco Square.
Good-quality food with superb panoramic views over Mouse Island.

MANDARIN PALACE Av. Paleokastritsa 4th klm, Sotiriotissa, Kontokali.
• 1200-1600, 1800-0100 daily. Bus no. 7, San Rocco Square, to Dassia.
The only Chinese restaurant on Corfu. Authentic Chinese food cooked by a Chinese chef!

SPIROS TAVERNA Benitses.
• 0900-1300, 1730-2330 daily. Bus no. 6 from San Rocco Square.
A family restaurant overlooking the bay with a mainly English menu.

RESTAURANT PIPILAS Kontokali.
• 0900-1130, 1230-1600, 1730-2330 daily. Bus no. 7.
Extensive menu offering Greek and English food. You can eat out on the vine-shaded patio.

TAVERNA OLYMPIA Moraitika.
• 0800-0200 daily. Moraitika bus from New Fortress Square.
A family-run restaurant with an extensive menu of Greek and English food.

XENIHTIS Potamou 12.
• 1900-0200 Mon.-Sat. Bus no. 4 from San Rocco Square.
A high-class gourmet restaurant serving mainly French dishes.

MAMMA LINA Nafsikas 18, Kanoni.
• 1300-1500, 2000-2400 daily. Bus no. 2 from the Esplanade.
A pleasant restaurant with an extensive menu of Italian and Greek food.

CALAMI BEACH Kalami.
• 0830-2400 daily. Kassiopi bus from New Fortress Square.
A simple beachside restaurant overlooking the bay, serving good food at reasonable prices.

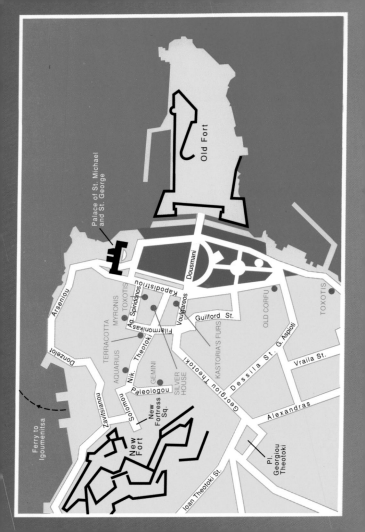

Gifts

GEMINI 50 Paleologou St.
•0830-1400, 1730-2100 Mon.-Fri., 0830-1400 Sat.
See the artist, Nicos Michalopoulos, working in his shop skilfully fashioning jewellery in gold, silver and wood from designs inspired by sea and sun.

TOXOTIS 12 Agiou Spiridonos St. and Corfu Palace Hotel.
•0930-2130 Mon.-Sat.
This jewellery shop run by Dimitrios Pagiatakis has an attractive and tempting window display.

AQUARIUS 95 Nik. Theotoki St.
•0900-2130 Mon.-Sat.
Pretty, feminine jewellery designed by Maria Roditi and hand crafted.

SILVER HOUSE 17 Nik. Theotoki St.
•1000-1400, 1630-2100 Mon.-Sat.
Venetian-inspired silver work, including jewellery and miscellaneous items. Workshop opposite.

MYRONIS 27 Filarmonikis St.
•0830-2130 daily.
High-quality olive wood carvings from family-run workshop.

TERRACOTTA 2 Filarmonikis St.
•0900-2300 Mon.-Sat. (summer), 0900-1430, 1730-2030 (winter).
Beautifully displayed handicrafts: ceramics, silk paintings, hand-blown glass, jewellery.

OLD CORFU 2 Kapodistriou St.
•1000-1400, 1700-2100 daily.
Exclusive art and antique shop, worth visiting for the artistic display.

KASTORIA'S FURS 17 Voulgareos St.
•0900-1300, 1700-2100 daily.
Large selection of fur goods.

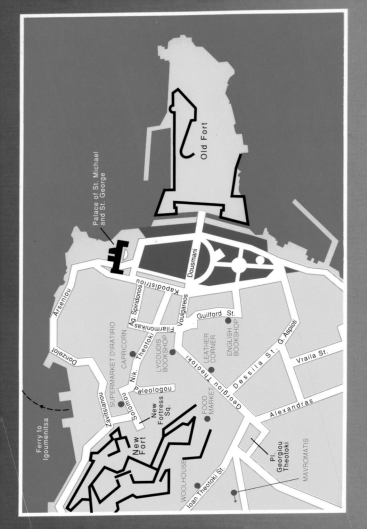

Miscellaneous

WOOLHOUSE 31 Ioan Theotoki (Avramiou).
•0830-1400, 1700-2030 daily.
Articles in pure Greek wool at reasonable prices and all made on the premises. Orders undertaken.

SUPERMARKET D'IRATIRIO 13 Solomou St.
•0830-1330 Mon., Wed., Sat., 0830-1330, 1830-2100 Tues., Thurs., Fri. Near the bus station.
Greek and European products in a conveniently situated supermarket.

FOOD MARKET Dessila St.
•Daily until 1330. Near the base of the New Fortress.
Lively, noisy, typically Greek market with colourful and attractive displays.

ENGLISH BOOKSHOP 40 Guilford St.
•0900-1330 Mon., Wed., Sat., 0830-1330, 1730-2030 Tues., Thurs., Fri.
Books (some antiquarian) in English, French and Italian.

LYCOUDIS BOOKSHOP 65 E Volgareos.
•0830-1400 Mon., Wed., 0830-1330, 1730-2030 Tues., Thurs., Fri., 0830-1330 Sat.
Best selection of English-language guide books and histories of Corfu.

THE LEATHER CORNER 4 Georgiou Theotoki.
•0900-2100 Mon.-Sat.
The largest stockists of leather goods on the island.

CAPRICORN 67a Nik. Theotoki St.
•0930-2130 Mon.-Sat.
Articles crafted by the owner in interesting fabrics such as wool, silk and leather knitted together plus caftans, hand painted shawls and silk items.

MAVROMATIS 13 km from Corfu Town on the Paleokastritsa road.
•Open in the mornings only.
*Factory and shop selling Greek spirits including Ouzo, brandy and Koum Kouat (see **Drinks**).*

Corfu Town

SPIANADA
In front of the Old Fortress.
Esplanade and elegant French-style arcade - the Liston. See **Cricket.**

PALACE OF ST MICHAEL AND ST GEORGE
•0845-1500 Mon.,Wed.-Sat., 0930-1430 Sun., hols. •400 Drs.
State rooms, the Museum of Asiatic Art, and public library. See **A-Z.**

OLD FORTRESS
•0800-1900. On eastern promontory of the town. •Free.
Venetian fortress which once housed the entire population. See **A-Z.**

SIR THOMAS MAITLAND'S BANDSTAND
Southern end of Spianada.
Built in memory of Sir Thomas Maitland. See **High Commissioners.**

STATUE OF SCHULENBERG
Central Avenue just before entering Old Fortress.
Commemorates a German mercenary, hired by the Venetians, and who successfully defended the city against the Turks in 1716.

STATUE OF ADAM
In front of Royal Palace.
Sir Frederick Adam (curiously attired in a toga). See **High Commissioners.**

TOWN HALL
Voulgareos St.
Splendid Venetian building, no public access. See **A-Z.**

NATIONAL LIBRARY
•0900-1400. Royal Palace, Spianada.
Built by Lord Guilford as a study centre for poets. Now a public library.

NEW FORTRESS
East of the Old Town.
Towers over Old Port concealing labyrinth of dark passages. No access.

MON REPOS
l.5 km south of town centre. Bus no. 2 (Kanoni) from Esplanade.
19thC villa, birthplace of Prince Philip (1921). Closed to the public.

CHURCH OF ST JASON AND ST SOSIPATROS
Just south of the town at Anemolilos in the bay of Garitsa.
Small 12thC Byzantine church of great interest. See **A-Z.**

MONASTERY OF PLATITERA
Near suburb of Mandouki.
Contains rare icons of post-Byzantine art. See **A-Z**.

PONTIKONISSI Kanoni Bay.
6 km south of town. Bus no. 2 (Kanoni) from Spianada; short boat trip.
'Mouse Island', twin islet of Vlacherna with 13thC chapel.

PALEOPOLIS BASILICA Opposite gates of Monrepos.
Oldest church in Corfu, originally constructed in 5thC AD.

MENECRATES TOMB
Take Kanoni road and turn right.
*Mound with a circular stone base once crowned with the magnificent
crouching lion which is now in the Archaeological Museum (see* **A-Z**).

TEMPLE OF ARTEMIS
Take the Kanoni road and turn right down a side road marked 'Stratia'.
Remains of one of the most important temples on the island. See **Gorgons.**

TEMPLE OF KARDAKI
Take Kanoni road and turn left about half-way along.
Remains of large hilltop sanctuary probably dedicated to Hera.

CONVENT OF VLACHERNA
•0900-1800. Southern tip of Kanoni promontory. Bus no. 2.
*Twin islet with Pontikonissi and joined to mainland by a jetty. Visit the l7thC
convent. Boats from here to Pontikonissi.*

Around the Island

MONASTERY OF PALEOKASTRITSA 24 km north west of Corfu Town.
•0700-1300, 1500-2000 daily. Bus from New Fortress Square. •Free.
13thC whitewashed Byzantine monastery. See EXCURSION 2, **Paleokastritsa.**

MONASTERY OF PANTOCRATOR 35 km north west of Corfu.
Turn left after Pyrgi to Strinilas, then two-hour walk.
Mountaintop monastery (906 m) built in 1347. See EXCURSION 1, WALK 1.

BENITSES
12.5 km south of Corfu Town.
Modern resort, but does have some Roman ruins. See EXCURSION 2.

ANGELOKASTRO CASTLE.
27 km north west of Corfu Town, via Krini.
13thC Byzantine castle perched on a hillside. See WALK 3, **Paleokastritsa.**

KASSIOPI 36 km north east of Corfu Town.
Nine buses daily from New Fortress Square.
Castle and church with 17thC frescoes. See BEACHES 1, EXCURSION 1, **A-Z.**

MORAITIKA AND MESSONGHI
19 km from Corfu Town on the south-east coast.
Greek temples in hills around Messonghi and Roman bath in Moraitika.

ACHILLION PALACE Gastouri Village.
•0800-1900 daily. Bus no.10 from San Rocco Square. •200 Drs.
Summer residence of the Empress Elizabeth. See EXCURSION 2, **A-Z.**

AGIOS MARKOS CHURCH Agios Markos.
16 km north of Corfu Town, near Pyrgi.
Built in 1075 with Cappadocian-style frescoes. See EXCURSION 1.

PERITHIA 46 km from Corfu Town.
On slopes of Mount Pantocrator. 2 or 3 buses a day from Kassiopi.
Almost deserted village with winding, cobbled streets. See WALK 1.

Roda

Perithia

Acharavi

Loutses

Kassiopi

Perithia

*Monastery
of Pantocrator*

Mount
Pantocrator

Strinilas

Sinies

Viglatsouri

Spartylas

Nissaki

Pyrgi

Corfu

Pantocrator/Perithia

A: *A climb from Strinilas to the top of Mount Pantocrator. Three hours each way.*

From Corfu Town drive north to Pyrgi, then take the road to the north which twists and turns slowly up through the mountainous region of Megalos Gremos through the picturesque mountain village of Spartylas (424 m) to Strinilas (30 km). Park your car here and then take the route to the top of Mount Pantocrator (906 m), crowned by a beautiful monastery (see **EXCURSION 1, SIGHTSEEING 3**). This is a fairly steep climb but the wonderful sweeping views over the island, the Greek mainland and, of course, the sea will reward your efforts!

B: *A walk to the old village of Perithia through the beautiful Greek country-side. One and a half hours each way.*

From Corfu Town drive to Kassiopi, then 6 km beyond the town turn left through the remains of an old archway. Drive through the village of Perithia and then on through the village of Loutses. About 1 km after Loutses leave the car where the road turns into a very stony track. Follow this track as it winds gradually upwards through the hills. Listen for the sound of goatbells and birdsong, and enjoy the profusion of wild flowers along the route. After about an hour you will see a cluster of small houses ahead which is the beginning of the village of old Perithia. Only a few inhabitants remain here now.
After wandering through the old streets of the village, return by the same route, which provides spectacular views of the mountains across in Albania.

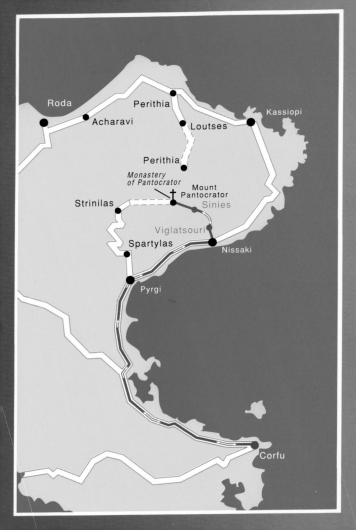

Old Sinies

Take the Kassiopi-Loutses-Perithia bus from New Fortress Square and alight at Viglatsouri, close to Nissaki. The walk is best done in the early morning or late afternoon to avoid the midday heat. It is advisable to wear a pair of strong shoes as the ground is quite rough in places.

A: *Two hours each way.*
After alighting from the bus walk along the concrete road named 'Viglatsouri' until it eventually becomes an overgrown, stony track which bends to the right in front of a small house. Follow the route down a wide, deep valley and across a dry stream bed then up the other side in a series of zig-zags then straight alongside a wall bordering some old terraces. Suddenly you will come across the abandoned village, its unoccupied houses with their empty windows and open doors giving it an eerie atmosphere. After exploring the village and wandering a little along the disused roads return to Nissaki along the same route, or continue the walk to Mount Pantocrator.

B: *Four hours each way from Nissaki.*
This walk from Old Sinies to the top of Mount Pantocrator is the most strenuous on the island and should only be undertaken by those who are fit and equipped with food (sandwiches, chocolate), water, good, strong walking shoes and a hat to avoid heatstroke. Tell a responsible person where you are going and keep an eye on the weather as clouds can descend very quickly.
The path from Old Sinies runs alongside the river bed before crossing it to start climbing its left bank. The path virtually disappears here so walkers will make their own way up through the terraces until arriving at a low ridge covered in shrubs and thorns. From here the route is quite clear. After following the path across the ridge you will see a steep valley stretching away in front of you. Ascend this valley, keeping to the right-hand slope and picking your way from a maze of steep paths which criss-cross each other until they converge at the head of the valley. This is very difficult terrain with loose soil, shale and plenty of thorn bushes!
Follow the path keeping the left-hand wall of a huge basin in view and,

when this becomes more difficult to see, aim for a prominent rock. Just before arriving at the rock you will come across the edge of the basin wall and a broken man-made wall surrounding an enclosure. Look carefully and you will see the faint outline of a path leading almost directly to the summit of the mountain and which becomes clearer as it climbs higher. Follow it upwards until arriving at a shepherd's hut; on the left here is a ruined wall, which you should climb over, and look again for the rather faint outlines of a path which begins near the wall. Do not follow the lower path as it does not lead to the mountaintop. From here the path becomes clearer until it meets the concrete road at the top which is used by cars making their way to the monastery and the mountaintop.

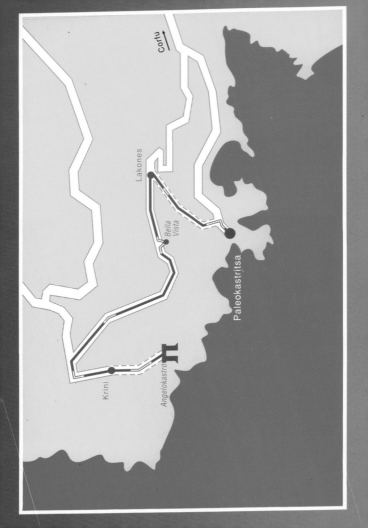

Corfu

Lakones

Bella
Vista

Krini

Angelokastro

Paleokastritsa

Paleokastritsa

There are regular buses to Paleokastritsa from New Fortress Square in Corfu Town, and it is reached by car through the village of Sgombos.

A: *One hour each way.*
After alighting at the bus terminal (or parking your car) near the shore-front, walk back a little way and turn left onto a road which is first gravel then, a little further on, concrete. Shortly after turning onto the track you will reach a fork. Take the right-hand path which begins to climb steadily past some houses until you reach a hand-painted wood-en sign marked 'Kakones'. Turn left at the sign and you will find your-self on a rough path made of large stones which winds its way upwards through olive groves to the village of Lakones. Some steps to the left lead up to the main street. Turn left from the main street and continue for approximately 1 km until you reach a small restaurant called the 'Bella Vista'. Relax and admire the spectacular view while taking some well-earned refreshment.

B: *One hour each way.*
If you wish to continue to Angelokastro (see **SIGHTSEEING 3, Paleokastritsa**) from the 'Bella Vista' continue along the road out of Lakones for approximately 1.5 km to the village of Krini. Walk through the village until the road becomes a track. Continue straight ahead (ignoring the path which descends to your left) through vineyards and groves of fig trees until you reach a T-junction. Follow the path to the left where it curves down and round the side of a hill, turns abruptly to face the castle, and climbs gently towards it. This ruined Byzantine cas-tle was built in the 13thC and named by Michael Komninos, a strange character from Byzantium, who transformed a dark cave into a chapel in honour of the Archangels Michael and Gabriel.

Accidents and Breakdowns: In the event of an accident follow the usual procedure of exchanging names, addresses and insurance details. The police are reluctant to intervene unless someone has been injured. For breakdowns contact the Greek Automobile and Touring Club (ELPA), tel: 104. They provide a free service to members of foreign auto clubs. There are agents for most makes of car in Corfu Town, and local mechanics are efficient and prices reasonable. See **Emergencies, Police**.

Accommodation: There are six official categories of hotels, ranging from the luxurious (Lux) to the very basic (E). The best value for money is often found in C/D family-run establishments. In high season it can be difficult to find hotel accommodation unless pre-booked. Contact travel agents or the NTOG (National Tourist Office of Greece) for a list of hotels on the island. There is no accommodation information service at the port or airport.

Private Houses: Categories A B C. No advance booking list available. At the port and airport people stand with cards advertizing rooms, usually C-class accommodation at about 1200-1400 Drs per night. The Tourist Police (tel: 30265) are also helpful when you are looking for somewhere to stay.

Tavernas: Categories D/E. Residents are usually expected to eat there also.

Villas and Apartments: Categories Lux, A , B. Self-catering accommodation let by the week (pre-booking usually essential).

Average prices for a double room with bath: Lux 4500-4700 Drs per night; category D 900-1300 Drs per night. Add 15% tax in high season and 10% for a stay of two nights or less. Breakfast is not included. There are often reductions for children. There is a room finding service at 43 Arseniou St., tel: 22102, open 0800-1000.

Youth Hostel: The only one on the island is in Kontaki village (7 km north of Corfu Town, bus no. 7), tel: 91202. It is for members only, but you can join on the spot.

Camping: There are 16 official camp sites with the usual facilities (a list is available at NTOG offices). The main season runs from April-October. Average prices: 135-150 Drs per person per day; 200-300 Drs for tent and car parking; 150-200 Drs for caravan. No unauthorized camping allowed.

Achillion: A palace built in 1891 for Empress Elizabeth of Austria and designed by Italian architect Cardita in Neoclassical style. It was purchased by Kaiser Wilhelm II of Germany in 1902 and used as a French military hospital during the First World War. It was restored in 1962 by Baron von Richthofen and converted into a casino (see **Nightlife**). A few mementoes of Elizabeth's time can be seen in the room next to her chapel on the ground floor, and some of the more interesting items amongst the clutter of statuary include a small statue of Byron and several busts of Greek philosophers. The most impressive piece is a huge bronze of the *Dying Achilles* on the northern terrace - which offers splendid open views - and these, together with the delightful gardens, compensate for the rather squat and vulgar architecture of the building. See **EXCURSION 2, SIGHTSEEING 3.**

Airport: 2 km south west of Corfu Town (tel: 30180 for information). There is no NTOG desk at the airport, but it does have all the usual facilities such as a bar, toilets, duty-free shops and exchange facilities. Olympic Airways run a bus into Corfu Town (50 Drs for everybody) and there are coach services to other parts of the island. There are also hotel shuttles for guests' use only. A taxi will cost 25 Drs per person and 30 Drs per km. Only use those equipped with a meter and insist that the driver uses it. It is roughly a 30-minute walk from the airport to Corfu Town.

Antiques: The export of antique icons and any other objects of historical interest found in the sea or elsewhere is strictly prohibited. See **SHOPPING 1.**

Archaeological Museum: The outstanding exhibit here is the Gorgon Pediment discovered in 1911 which dates from the early 6thC BC when it was part of the temple of Artemis in the ancient city of Corcyra. This enormous pediment (17 m wide and 3 m high) depicts a central, fascinatingly hideous figure of Medusa, one of the three Gorgons, (see **A-Z**) with a winged back and serpents writhing on her head and at her waist. She is flanked by her offspring Pegasus and Chrysaor and guarded by two lion-panthers. The remainder of the frieze is occupied by various mythological figures - gods, goddesses and animals. Almost equally impressive is the beautiful Corinthian statue of a crouching lion (7thC BC) said to come from the tomb of Menecrates (see **SIGHTSEEING 2**) and one of the finest animal sculptures of the Classical period. Other exhibits include temple decorations and bronzeware and a recent acquisition, a complete set of armour found in a local tomb, is also worth seeking out. See **CHURCHES & MUSUEMS.**

Baby-sitting: Ask at your hotel reception well in advance. The cost is around 300-500 Drs per hour. Corfu residents usually take their children out with them; and children are allowed in most establishments. See **Children**.

Barbecues: Usually organized by tour operators (eg Thomson,

Intasun) and take place on beaches that can only be reached by local caique or small hire-boats. The most popular venue is Linopoulos, on the east coast towards Kassiopi, which is always crowded.

Beaches: Bathing is not recommended around Corfu Town because of pollution, but of course there are plenty of safe and clean beaches within a short distance. In general, beaches facing the Greek mainland are usually shingle, whereas those on the west coast are sandy (and very crowded in summer). Try those where access is more difficult, for example by moped or boat. Nude bathing is prohibited, but tolerated on the more isolated beaches around the island.
See BEACHES 1, BEACHES 2.

Best Buys: The National Welfare Organization is now actively encouraging the revival of many of the old Greek folk arts and crafts and visitors are welcome to watch the craftsmen and women at work. Crafts include pottery, leatherwork, weaving, olive wood carving, copperware, embroidery, and gold and silver work. Fine, hand-crafted jewellery often echoes designs of ancient times - Minoan, Mycenian and Macedonian. Fur (from Kastoria) is also a good buy (see SHOPPING 1). Shops often allow visitors to reserve an item by paying a small deposit and settling the balance once back home. The main shopping area stretches from the Liston (see SIGHTSEEING 1) to the Old Town Port.
See BEST BUYS, SHOPPING.

Birdwatching: Mainly a winter activity when birds can be sighted at the lagoon near the airport (sea birds, heron, duck, *etc*), Lake Korission (a protected area) on the Lefkimmi road on the west coast, and at Antinioti on the north coast between Kassiopi and Roda.

Boat Services: The port terminal has few facilities and is not very clean. There is a Bureau de Change (tel: 30481), and the ticket agencies are sited below Donzelot Parade, on the left-hand side of the Old Port.
Ferries: Hellenic Mediterranean Lines (open 0730-1330, 1730-2030. Tel: 39747) run services to Brindisi and Patras.

Ionian Lines, Epirus Lines and Fragline are at 74, 76 and 50 Xen. Stratigou St., New Port.
Vikentios Manessis Travel. Tel: 32664.
Corfu-Saudi Travel, 46 Xen Straitgou St. Tel: 25003 - services to Brindisi, Bari, Ancona and Venice.
There are also services from Kavos (on the south coast) to Paxi at 0930 Mon., Tues., Fri. and Sat.
See **ISLANDS.**

Bouzouki: Musical instrument originating in Orient and brought to Greece by refugees in 1922. Banned by the authorities at one time, it continued to be played in underground clubs and has seen a great revival in its popularity over recent years. For many people it seems to characterize the essence of Greek music.

Budget: Examples of typical prices are given below - these prices will be much higher in up-market establishments such as those in the Liston (see **SIGHTSEEING 1**).
Hotel breakfast: 120-180 Drs.
Restaurant lunch: 500-800 Drs.

Coffee (instant): 40-70 Drs.
Beer: 60-80 Drs.
Soft drink: 45-50 Drs.
Greek brandy: 50-90 Drs.

Buses: There are two bus services: *City Buses* run from the terminal at
San Rocco Square (open from 0730-2130), including services to
Achillion (no. 10); Benitses (no. 6); Dassia (no. 7); and Pelekas (no. 11).
The bus to Kanoni leaves from the Esplanade. The service is reasonable
but buses can get crowded. The standard fare is 35 Drs per journey,
which you pay on the bus.
Island Services run from the coach station in front of New Fortress, Old
Port. Drivers tend to go rather fast and the coaches vary in age from the
ancient to relatively modern, but are safe and clean. Fares range from
120-200 Drs. Schedules are printed in the *Corfu News* and are available at the NTOG office. There is no night service.
Bus services to Athens: 0630, 0900 and 1830 from New Fortress bus
station. Tickets should be purchased the day before your journey. The
ferry ticket (which is not included in the price) should be purchased
from office no. 7 in the port 15 minutes before departure. The last bus
arrives in the outskirts of Athens at 0530; from here take a no. 51 bus to
Omonia Square.

Cameras and Photography: Most makes of film, batteries, video
tapes and accessories are available in Corfu, but are expensive. Films
and batteries are obtainable in most supermarkets outside Corfu Town
but not video accessories. Several shops offer rapid developing but the
quality varies. Photography is allowed in museums but tripods and
flash are not.

Car Hire: Several car hire companies operate around the island but
they are expensive, as is petrol. Some companies refuse drivers under
25. Officially an International Driving Licence is essential but many
operators accept a domestic licence if issued more than 12 months ago.
Credit card payment may give reductions or replace payment of a
deposit.

Chemists: Look for the sign with a red cross on a white background. They open 0815-1330 Mon., Wed., Sat., 0815-1330, 1715-2030 Tues., Thurs., Fri., and at other times on a rota basis - enquire at your hotel or ask the Tourist Police (tel: 30265). Prescriptions are needed for treatments for stomach problems and for sleeping pills. See **Health**.

Children: The Greeks are very fond of children and they are accepted (and welcome) in most establishments. There are two recreation parks in Corfu Town with swings, slides, roundabouts and climbing frames: the best is opposite the cricket pitch, next to the Old Fortress; the other is at Garitsa on the Kanoni road, and is not so well kept. Most resorts and hotel complexes offer organized activities for children. If a child is lost contact the Tourist Police (tel: 30265) or the local village police, but remember that the latter may speak little or no English. See **Baby-sitting**.

Church of St Jason and St Sosipatros: A small but very beautiful Byzantine church built in the 12thC. The church is dedicated to

two of St Paul's disciples (represented in the church by two fine 16thC icons) who brought Christianity to the island in the 2ndC AD. The fascinating red tile design on the outer walls has been recognized as Cufic lettering (an early form of Arabic writing, much used in decoration) and the octagonal cupola rests on three ancient monolithic pillars. Finally the church is surrounded by a well-tended garden which is full of flowers. See SIGHTSEEING 2.

Church of St Spyridon: A surprisingly simple and relatively unadorned church (built 1589-1596) dedicated to Corfu's much-loved patron saint, St Spyridon, after whom many boys are named (Spiros). The painted ceiling, a 19thC copy of an earlier work, depicts the Saint's miracles, and a cluster of 18thC silver hanging lamps and candelabra gleam in the dim light. There is also a fine wrought iron screen on the gallery. The mummified body of the saint is kept in a small, dark sanctuary near the altar, which is lit by votive candles and guarded by two priests. The splendid sarcophagus, a gilt casket lavishly embellished with jewels and contained in a silver outer case, is opened and carried upright around the town four times a year. See CHURCHES & MUSEUMS, Events, St Spyridon.

Climate: It is not always sunny - more rain falls here than on the Greek mainland and in spring it can be quite wet. By May, however, it is warm with plenty of sunshine (19°C-24°C); from June to September it is hot and dry (18°C-35°C), but cool sea breezes allow comfortable nights. Autumn brings occasional thunderstorms but generally good weather (16°C-22°C) and winters are rainy and cool (5°C -12°C) although snow is practically unknown.

Consulates:
Great Britain - 11 Alexandra Av, Corfu Town. Tel: 30055.
USA - 91 Vas. Sofias Av, 11521 Athens. Tel: 721-2951/9.
Australia - 37 Dimitriou Soutso, Athens. Tel: 644-7303.
Canada - 4 Ioann. Gennadiou St., Athens. Tel: 723-9511.
Republic of Ireland - 7 Vas. Konstandinou Av, Athens. Tel: 721-2951.
New Zealand - 15-17 Tsocha St., Athens. Tel: 641-0311-5.

Conversion Charts:

TEMPERATURE

°C −30 −25 −20 −15 −10 −5 0 5 10 15 20 25 30 35 40 45
°F   −20 −10 0 10 20 30 40 50 60 70 80 90 100 110

DISTANCE

kms   0 1 2 3 4 5 6   8   10   12   14   16
miles 0 ½ 1 1½ 2   3   4   5   6   7   8   9   10

WEIGHT

grams 0 100 200 300 400 500 600 700 800 900 1 kg
ounces 0   4   8   12 1 lb 20   24   28 2 lb

Cricket: Brought to the island by the British in 1864 and very popular. The main pitch is on the Esplanade in Corfu Town and matches are played here on Wed. and Sun., starting at 1500. There are two clubs and a cricket festival in September with teams from England and Malta.

Crime and Theft: There is very little crime on the island but you should always leave your valuables in the hotel safe. If something is stolen, inform your hotel manager and the police (tel: 38568).

Culture: *Customs and traditions:* The Organization of Corfiot Cultural Activities is reviving customs such as the Varcarola and the Carnival. *Music:* Corfu Town supports a Philharmonic Orchestra and Choir which perform abroad and there are 11 others around the island, some of the largest are at Korakianas, Skripero, Gastoyriou and Koinopiaston. *Singing and dancing:* The Choir of Kerkyra, the Kerkyraiki Kandata and Kerkyraiki Mantolinata give classical performances at the Kerkyraikko Chorogramma. The Laodamas group offer more traditional dancing. *Theatre:* The Kerkyraiki Kallitechniki Skini theatre group perform annually. *Sound and Light Show:* Daily shows, re-telling Greek history followed by folk dancing, from 15 May - 30 Sept. 2145-2230 at the Old Fortress. Tickets from the NTOG office.

Currency: The unit of Greek currency is the drachma (Dr). Coins are 1, 2, 5, 10, 20 and 50 Drs (the design is changing so there are currently different 1, 2 and 50 Dr coins). Notes are issued in denominations of 50, 100, 500, 1000 and 5000 Drs. See **Money**.

Customs:

Duty Paid Into:	Cigarettes	or	Cigars	or	Tobacco	Spirits	Wine
E.E.C.	300		75		400 g	1.5 l	5 l
U.K.	300		75		400 g	1.5 l	5 l

Danilia Village: The village was built by the Bouas family as an authentic reconstruction of a typical Corfiot community, in respect of architecture, customs and so on. Among the attractions are: St Irene's church in the square; a traditional olive press; and the Folk Museum with displays depicting everyday life in the past. There is also a shopping centre selling Corfiot crafts (see **BEST BUYS**) and lively evening entertainment with folk dancing and singing and a set dinner menu including free wine. See **NIGHTLIFE**.

Drinks: *Wines:* the best-known is *retsina*, a white wine flavoured with pine resin and best drunk ice-cold (it also helps to digest the oil in Greek food). Other reasonable-quality wines include those from Kephalonia and Mount Athos, and most regions produce their own varieties. *Ouzo* is an aniseed-flavoured spirit served with water. *Brandies:* Metaxa, Botrys and Cambas are three fairly palatable Greek brandies. *Spirits:* imported spirits are much more expensive than Greek spirits which are fine for mixing. *Beer:* Greek beer is brewed like lager - Greek brands to try are Fix and Hellas. Imported beer is also widely available. *Fruit juices:* there is a good selection. *Water:* tap water is drinkable and mineral water is widely available.

Driving: It is essential to have an EC or International Driving Licence, third party insurance and a national identity sticker on the rear of your car. Green card insurance is also recommended. Drive on the right, overtake on the left, and give priority to traffic from the right unless otherwise indicated. The use of horns in towns is (theoretically) prohibited and seat belts are compulsory. Traffic conditions are generally good except in Corfu Town in high season; main roads are usually tarred but there can be potholes and roads tend to be unstable at the edges; there are not many signs indicating bends or other potential hazards, but plenty of goats, chickens and dogs roaming freely. It is best to drive slowly and expect the unexpected!
Parking: There is one free car park in Corfu Town, otherwise spaces are limited. Illegal parking results in a fine or removal of numberplates which can be difficult to retrieve.
Petrol: Petrol stations are plentiful in Corfu Town but scarce elsewhere.

They normally close at 1900 but there is always one open all night on a rota basis - telephone the police on 100 for details.

Drugs: Not tolerated. Possession of small quantities can result in imprisonment and a fine. Trafficking can mean life imprisonment.

Eating Out: For a quick snack local shops sell doughnuts (*oukoumaes*), cheese pies (*typoites*), sausage rolls, spinach pies (*anakoites*), and pizzas. For Greek fast-food try *souvlaki*, barbecued meat served in pitta bread with salad and yoghurt. For more elaborate meals there are plenty of eating-places to suit all tastes. See **RESTAURANTS**, **Food**, **Restaurants**.

Electricity: Two-pin plugs, 220 volts/50 Hz. Adapters are available in most electrical retailers.

Emergencies:
Police - Tel: 100.
Ambulance - Tel: 30562/30033.
Fire - Tel: 199.
Tourist Police - Tel: 30265.
See **Accidents and Breakdowns**, **Chemists**, **Health**.

Events: *January:* Traffic Police receive gifts from motorists, and children also receive presents; 6: Epiphany, Blessing of the Waters, children dive into the bay in front of the Nautical Club to look for a cross previously blessed by the Bishop. *February:* Two-week Carnival with masked balls and dressing up for the children who hit each other with plastic batons. *Mardi Gras Sunday:* Parade in Corfu Town with fancy dress and huge floats. In Episkepsis the priests dance slowly and solemnly through the village to the sound of chanting. *Clean Monday:* The first day of Lent and usually celebrated by family picnic-outings. *Good Friday:* Decorated bier with Christ's body carried in a silent procession through the streets. *Easter Saturday:* At 11 am residents throw a piece of pottery from their windows. This strange custom is peculiar to Corfu and is thought to symbolize the casting out of Judas. In the evening the

Bishop celebrates Mass on the Spianada and at midnight church bells ring, firework shows begin and everyone lights a candle. *1 May*: Families make for the coast to picnic in cars brightly decorated with flowers. *21 May:* Union Day (marks the union of the Ionian Islands with Greece when the British left on 21 May 1864) with a parade and cannons, and a performance of the Corfu Town Philharmonic Orchestra near the Liston. *28 October*: Soldiers and schoolchildren parade to commemorate rejection of Mussolini's ultimatum in 1940 which then involved Greece in the Second World War. *12 December*: St Spyridon's feast day. All males named Spyridon receive a gift and the saint's body is exposed for three days so that devotees may kiss its velvet slipper.

St Spyridon processions: These commemorate the miracles performed by the saint and take place on 11 August (saved island from Turks); first Sunday in November and Palm Sunday (saved island twice from plague); Saturday of Holy Week (saved island from famine). There are colourful processions through the streets following the saint's relics in the gilt casket (see **Church of St Spyridon, St Spyridon**).

Village saints' days or Panighiri: Churches are specially decorated and residents go to the central square after morning Mass; lambs are roasted on spits, bands play and there is singing, dancing and eating until nightfall. The following list is a guide: Paleokastritsa - Friday after Easter; Analipsis - Ascension Day; Lakones and Kastellani - Whit Sunday; Nymphes - 21 May; Petreli - 2 July; Agios Prokopios and Kavos - 8 July; Magonlades - 20 July; Mount Pantocrator - 3-6 Aug.; Pontikonissi - 6 Aug.; Mandouki - 14 Aug.; Myrtiotissa - 24 Sept.

Food: Popular Greek dishes are: *moussaka* (minced meat, aubergines, potatoes and béchamel sauce); *souvlaki* (chunks of meat cooked on a spit, like kebabs); *pastitsio* (minced meat, macaroni and béchamel sauce); spit-roasted lamb and pork. Specialities from Corfu include: *sofrito* (veal casserole in white sauce seasoned with onions and garlic); *bourdeto* (fish casserole with onions and red pepper); *pastitsada* (veal cooked in tomato sauce with pasta). Fish is always fresh and available everywhere - cooked over charcoal, fried or in soup. Try the more exotic varieties such as octopus, squid and crispy fried *calamari*. Lobster is delicious but very expensive. See **Eating Out**, **Restaurants**.

Gorgons: In Greek mythology the Gorgons were the three sisters of the Graeae - Medusa, Stheno and Euryale - represented as old women with only one eye and one tooth between them. In spite of these handicaps Medusa, the only mortal one, slept with Poseidon and was, as a punishment, turned into a winged monster with writhing snakes for hair and a look that turned the beholder to stone. Perseus tricked and beheaded her and the winged horse Pegasus and the warrior Chrysaor came to life from her spilled blood. Her head was later fixed on Athena's shield.

Hairdressers: Approximate prices for shampoo and set/blow dry are: men 400-650 Drs + 10% tip; women 1150 Drs + 10% tip.

Health: Visitors are strongly advised to take out personal medical insurance before leaving home. Residents of EC member countries are treated free (UK residents should obtain form E 111 from the Department of Social Security before travelling abroad) but the health

Useful numbers:
General Hospital (with 24-hour emergency service): Aghia Irini, Konstanta St. Tel: 30562/39403. Ambulance service is prompt and efficient (see **Emergencies**).
Clinics: 1 Ethniki Paleokastritsa. Tel: 36044; 38 Markora St. Tel: 32686.
English-speaking doctor: Thanasis Michalopoulos, 23a Ioan. Theotaki St. Tel: 37540/34206.
English-speaking dentist: Michalis Valmas, 9 Evangelistrias. Tel: 30458.
In general, standards of hygiene on the island are good; fair-skinned visitors should take care at first in the sun, particularly in the summer. Many inexperienced riders are involved in accidents on hired mopeds and motorbikes, so take care. See **Chemists.**

High Commissioners: All the Ionian Islands came under British protection between 1814 and 1863 and there were ten High Commissioners (one of whom was Gladstone). The first two were the most noteworthy: Sir Thomas Maitland, the first High Commissioner and much disliked by the Corfiots after he refused to allow Corfu to take part in the War of Independence against the Turks in 1821 - there is an Ionian-style bandstand named after him on the Spianada (see SIGHTSEEING 1); and Sir Frederick Adam the second High Commissioner, who was responsible for helping to design a system of aqueducts to bring water to Corfu Town. These aqueducts are still functioning today. He was also responsible for building the villa Monrepos (see SIGHTSEEING 2). There is a statue of Sir Frederick, dressed somewhat incongruously in a toga, in front of the Royal Palace (see SIGHTSEEING 1).

Ithaca: One of the smallest of the Ionian Islands (approx. 29 km by 6 km with a population of about 6500, a third of whom live in the capital, Ithaca Town or Vathi) but with considerable traditional character, extremely helpful and friendly residents, and still relatively unspoilt by tourism. The island is separated from its larger neighbour Kephalonia by a wide channel and the ferry service to Ithaca is connected with that to Kephalonia. Roads on the island can be very rough but there is a bus service and taxis are available. The main ferry terminus is at Ithaca Town (Vathi) on the east coast, its dazzling white houses clinging to the

hillside overlooking the deep U-shaped Bay of Molos. This mountainous yet lush island is reputedly the birthplace of Odysseus and it is said that he hid the gifts given to him by the Phaeacians in the Cave of the Nymphs or Marble Cave (3 km north of Ithaca Town). Further north is Kathara Monastery built 600 m above sea level with outstanding views from the bell tower. Stavros (19 km north west of Ithaca Town) is a friendly, rural village with taverna accommodation and is an excellent starting point from which to explore the north of the island including the Bay of Polis (20 min towards the coast from Stavros) with its tiny quay, colourful local fishing boats and legendary sunken city. Nearby is another cave, Loizos cave, where archaeologists discovered fragments of pottery indicating the worship of Artemis, Hera and Athena. Pelikata (1 km north of Stavros) is the site of another excavation which confirmed the existence of a Bronze Age settlement (from 2200 BC) and strengthens the claim that the ancient city of Ithaca was built in the area. Frikes and Kioni (16 km and 20 km north east of Ithaca Town) are peaceful, unassuming and typically Ionian seaside villages. A trip to this little island is well worth considering and a day trip could be included in a visit to Kephalonia. Accommodation is scarce but there are a few hotels (try Mendor Hotel, Ithaca Town, tel: 0674 32433) and some rooms are available in tavernas and private houses.
See **ISLANDS**.

Kassiopi: Despite recent development as a tourist resort, this friendly seaside village still retains considerable character and individuality - as well it might considering its past importance as a flourishing port visited by such eminent people as Cicero, Cato and Nero, who reputedly gave one of his last recitals here. The 13thC hillside fortress, now ruined, is a reminder of Kassiopi's past significance and well worth a visit, as is the Panagia Kassiotropi Church with its 17thC frescoes. To the north of Kassiopi are unspoilt beaches of white sand and pebbles.
See **BEACHES 1, EXCURSION 1, SIGHTSEEING 3**.

Kephalonia: Mountainous and majestic, the largest of the Ionian Islands looms dramatically and unforgettably from the sea. This 737 km² island is home to 31,000 inhabitants most of whom live

around the main town, Argostolion, 23 km west of Sami, the ferry terminus and usual point of arrival. Sami has little to commend it but try
to see the Roman remains with frescoes just outside the town. West of
Sami are the underground sea caves of Melissani and Drogorati (the
Fiscardo bus will take you within a short walk of the caves - about 30
min drive). Agia Efimia (10 km north of Sami) is a delightful fishing port
with good restaurants. A severe earthquake in 1953 virtually destroyed
the old town of Argostolion (west of Sami), founded by the Venetians in
1757, which has been rebuilt on a rather unimaginative grid pattern;
there is an archaeological museum (mainly Mycenian artefacts), a folk
museum and a cathedral with beautiful icons to see here. The famous
Katavrothes (swallow holes) are just 2.5 km from Argostolion and are a
rare geological phenomenon where the sea seems to disappear underground; in fact it crosses under the island and reappears at Melissani
(see above) where it once emerged with such a powerful force that it
was used to operate two mills! Other interesting sites accessible from
Argostolion include: Kastro (5 km), the former island capital, its old
buildings lying in ruins on the hillside and crowned with a hilltop castle - this Greek and Venetian town was destroyed by an earthquake in
1636. Lord Byron once stayed in Metaxata (9 km) where you will find
some Mycenian tombs and a ruined temple. Lakithra (10 km) also has
some Mycenian tombs and is the richest, most fertile area in the region.
Maxacarata (18 km) has a necropolis with several Mycenian tombs.
The Castle of St George (25 km, near Peratata) built by the Venetians in
1504 is very atmospheric with sweeping views; just beneath it is the
Agios Andreos monastery with its outstanding collection of icons.
North of Argostolion is Lixourion, a peaceful old-fashioned town where
you will find vestiges of the ancient city of Pali and a folk museum in
an old mansion; there are good beaches to the south. The late 16thC
castle in the delightful village of Assos (67 km north of Lixourion) was
built by the Venetians to protect the inhabitants from pirate raids.
Fiscardo (56 km north of Assos) is a quiet l2thC fishing port looking
across to Ithaca and protected by a dense forest of cypress trees.
Kephalonia will amply reward a stay of three days - there are hotels in
Argostolion, Sami, and Poros. Access by ferry, air (from Athens). Buses
operate throughout the island. Motorbike and scooter hire tends to be

expensive as only larger engines can handle the steep terrain. See **ISLANDS**.

Laundries: Hotel laundry service takes two to three days in high season. Self-service laundries are scarce - try Europa Hotel Self-Service, tel: 39304. Cost: approximately 500 Drs wash and dry.

Lefkada: 32 km by 12 km; population 25,000. With its densely covered mountainsides, vast golden beaches and picturesque villages Lefkada must be everyone's idea of a typical Greek island! Access is by bus from Athens (across the bridge which spans the narrow channel separating Lefkada from the mainland) or by boat from Kephalonia, Kioni and Ithaca. Lefkada Town is small and picturesque (population 6500) situated in the north of the island and built on a natural harbour overlooking a huge lagoon; note the brightly coloured wooden houses here and be sure to visit the castle of Santa Maura, founded in 1300 by John Orsini, a Frankish knight. Two churches are worth seeing: Agios Dimitrios which has four paintings by Panaghiotis Doxaras; and Agios Minas which contains ceiling paintings by Nicolas Doxaras. An archaeological museum at 21 Phaneromenis St. displays finds from the Bronze Age to Roman times. Interesting trips from Lefkada might include the ruins of Old Lefkada (polygonal enclosure, theatre and acropolis) 3 km from Lefkada on Nidri road and Nidri (18 km south of Kefkas on the east coast), a popular holiday resort and fishing port, and erstwhile home of the German archaeologist Dorpfeld (who claimed that Lefkada was Homer's Ithaca), now a museum. Look across from here to the islets of Scorpio, Scorpios, Sparti and Madouri. There is a good bathing beach (shingle) at the peaceful village of Poros (11 km south of Nidri); wander along its narrow, winding lanes and explore the old church with its l7thC painting of the Virgin. Earlier frescoes (15thC) adorn the church of Agios Georgios de Bisa at Marandochori (33 km from Lefkada. The fishing village of Vassiliki (40 km from Lefkada) has a pleasant, shady quay and extensive shingle beach and boat trips (*caique*) leave from here to several small islands. The lighthouse at Lefkata (58 km from Lefkada) stands on the site of the once world-famous shrine to Apollo and here, too, it is said that Sappho, rejected

by her beloved Phaona, leapt to her death from the cliffs. For a glimpse of traditional, rural island life visit the village of Karia (76 km from Lefkada) and stroll along its twisting, crowded lanes, enjoying the pretty gardens. There are many picturesque country walks that will take you to the heart of the island. Allow two or three days to enjoy Lefkada - accommodation ranges from hotels to camp sites (try the Lefkada Hotel, 2 Panagou St., Lefkada Town, tel: 0645 23916). Transport includes buses, taxis, and moped and scooter hire. See **ISLANDS**.

Lost Property: Contact the Lost Property Office, tel: 39294.

Markets: The food market (north of San Rocco Square) offers plenty of choice including Greek specialities and a full range of other European products. See **SHOPPING 2**.

Monastery of Platitera: An enchanting l7thC monastery (north west of Corfu town) set in a small white courtyard with pink stone walls. The lofty bell tower is Venetian but the buildings are traditional Greek style; be sure to visit the church and see the fine carved wooden screen and the icon of the Virgin Mary which was presented by Count John Capodistrias, first President of independent Greece (1827-1831), whose tomb can also be found here. There are some well-preserved examples of the Cretan school of painting at the rear of the church. See **SIGHTSEEING 2**.

Money: Banks: National Bank of Greece, Ev Voulgareos St., Corfu Town. Tel: 39357; Commercial Bank of Greece, Ev Voulgareos St., Corfu Town. Tel: 38489; Credit Bank of Greece, 4 Ag Dimitriou, Corfu Town. Tel: 38112. Traveller's cheques may be changed at banks, *bureaux de change* and Post Offices. Many shops will also accept traveller's cheques in the more common currencies such as US dollars, pounds sterling, French francs and deutschmarks . A passport is essential when changing money anywhere. In high season some *bureaux de change* are open up to ten hours per day, but there is no 24-hour service. Any theft or loss of money should be reported to the Tourist Police (tel: 30265) then contact your consulate (see **Consulates**).

Motorbike and Moped Hire: Motorbikes and mopeds are a very popular form of transport and there are hire shops all over the island. Prices vary widely: from 1500 Drs per day for motorbikes and from 200-300 Drs per day for bicycles. Mopeds are the ideal way to explore the islands. Fuel is sold from small, glass-topped pumps and approx. 300 Drs will fill the tank. Unfortunately many visitors are involved in accidents, mainly due to inexperience and poor road conditions. Insurance is included in hire charges and a passport or driving licence is usually held as a deposit.

Museum of Asiatic Art: Housed in the State Rooms in the West Wing of the Royal Palace of St Michael and St George (see **A-Z**), the collection comprises more than 10,000 pieces of oriental art dating from Neolithic times to the l9thC. It was formed by Gregory Manos, a Greek diplomat and scholar who offered the collection to the state in 1917 and died, relatively impoverished, 11 years later. The Manos collection was augmented by another diplomat, Nickolaos Hadzivasileion, who donated bronzes, screens and sculptures from Nepal, Tibet, India, Thailand, Korea and Japan. The main collection extends from Chinese pottery and porcelain from ancient to modern times, tomb figures and bronzes to a Japanese collection with books, prints, masks and weapons. See **CHURCHES & MUSEUMS.**

Music: Brass bands perform at the bandstand at the south end of the Esplanade on summer Saturday evenings (around 2100). There is lively *bouzouki* music (*rebetiza*) in the clubs on 'The Strip', but drinks and broken plates are expensive! Corfu Festival takes place annually in September and October with ballet, opera and classical music performed by visiting companies. Corfu Town has a Philharmonic Orchestra which, with its choir, performs abroad.
See **Culture**, **Nightlife**.

Nature: *Vegetation*: 3,500,000 olive trees produce Corfu's main crop and yield olives every second year from the beginning of November to the following spring. The cypress, the second most common tree, is a conifer with exceptionally hard wood and dense dark foliage - a sharp contrast to the olive, an evergreen with narrow leaves. The vine is not extensively cultivated and although most fruits grow readily only the orange and lemon are commercially produced. Wide areas of the island are completely overgrown by kermes oak, myrtle, arbutus, lentisk and a profusion of aromatic plants. Lawrence Durrell's *Prospero's Cell* and Gerald Durrell's *My Family and Other Animals* contain vivid descriptions of Corfu's countryside.

Wildlife: mammals resident include foxes, jackals, weasels, moles, hedgehogs, dormice and hares. Reptiles include tortoises, frogs, toads, lizards and snakes (most harmless). There is a wide variety of birdlife, including some rare species of white barn owl, and herons and king-fishers can occasionally be spotted (see **Birdwatching**). *Flowers:* the anemone opens the season in mid-January and by February/March Corfu's most stunning display is well under way. By the time the Judas trees blossom in May the show is in full swing and lasts until the end of June. The last flower of the year is the snowdrop in November. Corfu's heavier rainfall means that flowers, both wild and cultivated, grow abundantly and the scent from the flowering trees - wisteria, myrtle, oleander, lemon and orange - is sometimes almost overpowering.

Newspapers: Foreign newspapers and periodicals are available (one day after publication) in kiosks and shops all over Corfu. Two English language newspapers printed in Greece are *Athens News*, a daily with Greek and world news and television programmes, and *Corfu News*, a free monthly newspaper (April-October), which carries events listings with up-to-date information.

Nightlife: There's always plenty to do at night, from sitting on the café terraces sipping a cool drink and watching the world go by, to tak-ing part in organized outings by tour operators. These might include dinner, dancing and entertainment and are usually good value (see **Danilia Village**). The most popular discos are on what is known as 'The Strip', just north of Corfu Town where you'll find 'Playboy', 'La Boom', 'Apocalypsis', 'Hippodrome', and 'Bora Bora': entrance is usually around 1000 Drs which entitles you to a free drink. Once inside drinks prices vary, but you will find a wide choice available including local brands. Closing time is 0200 on weekdays and 0300 at weekends. Try the *bouzouki* bars in Gouvia for a change: 'Esperida', 'Alikos' and 'Corfu by Night' all provide good entertainment but can be expensive. For video bars try 'Black and White Bar', 6 Agios Vasila or 'Mermaid', 9 Agios Panton St.
There are three cinemas in Corfu which often show English and other European films with Greek subtitles: Pallas, G. Theotoki St. (near San

Rocco Square); Orpheus, Akadimias St.; Nausika, Marasali St. (open-air). The casino (*roulette, chemin de fer, baccarat* and *vingt-et-un*) is on the first floor of the Achillion Palace (see SIGHTSEEING 3, **A-Z**) and is open daily from 1900-0200. Evening wear and a passport are essential. See NIGHTLIFE, RESTAURANTS, **Culture**.

Old Fortress: Built by the Venetians in 1550, although some sections dating from a much earlier period already existed, this formidable structure stands on two levels to the east of Corfu Town, separated from it by an artificial moat and thus in an ideal defensive position. In fact the town's entire population lived within its walls from the 6th-13thC! Today its architectural features reflect the British occupation during Victoria's reign. It served as a military hospital from 1836-64 and again in the First World War. Now a military academy (open to the public; no photography) it also serves as a venue for the summer sound and light show (see **Culture**) and Corfu Ballet performances. See SIGHTSEEING 1.

Olive Wood Carving: This is one of Corfu's traditional crafts in which the artist shapes the articles by following the natural lines and

curves in the wood. The wood must be stored and dried for at least four years so that it will not split and natural flaws in the wood mean a great deal of waste.

Opening Times: *Shops:* 0800-1330, 1700-2030 Tues., Thurs., Fri. *Banks:* 0800-1400, 1615-1800 or 1730-1945 Mon.-Fri. Shops and banks are closed on Sundays and Bank Holidays.

Orientation: Corfu island is 50 km by 27 km with a population of approximately 93,000, almost a third of whom live in Corfu Town (Kerkyra) which is on the east coast, and the only sizeable town on the island. Corfu Town has been highly developed as a tourist resort and can be busy and noisy but there are also quiet, winding streets and gracious old buildings to see. To the north the island is mountainous with attractive villages such as Kassiopi (see **A-Z**) and Roda offering good bathing in clear blue water (see **BEACHES 1, EXCURSION 1**). To the south the island is much lower and villages such as Kavos with its sandy beach and shallow water are becoming increasingly popular. The most popular, lively (and noisy!) resorts (such as Benitses) will be found on the east coast. Invest in a good map as soon as you arrive. All road and street signs are in Greek.

Palace of St Michael and St George: (Royal Palace). This fine Classical and colonnaded building on the north edge of the Esplanade was constructed between 1819 and 1823 from stone shipped from Malta and intended as a residence for the British Lord High Commissioners. The frieze on the facade represents the emblems of the Ionian Islands. The rooms are airy and spacious with superb marble fireplaces, and those in the eastern wing have glorious sea views. Note particularly the handsome staircase in the entrance hall. The State Rooms are open to visitors and the Palace now houses the Museum of Asiatic Art (see **CHURCHES & MUSUEMS, A-Z**). See **SIGHTSEEING 1**.

Paleokastritsa: Six small coves washed by unbelievably clear blue water (a paradise for divers) and lined with strips of sand, the whole set against a dramatic background of sea caverns, tree-covered hills and cliffs. It is small wonder that Paleokastritsa is the best known and, unfortunately, one of the most crowded beach resorts on the island (particularly as the access road from Corfu Town is one of the island's best - constructed by British army engineers 150 years ago!). It is, however, well worth a visit if only to see the 13thC Byzantine monastery clinging tenaciously to a promontory far above sea level (see SIGHTSEE-ING 3). There are wonderful views from the monastery which once served as a military outpost (note the early-18thC Russian gun outside) and later as a British military convalescent hospital. Look offshore to the strange Kolouri rock, said to be the Phaeacian ship which took Ulysses home to Ithaca after his wanderings and petrified by the angry sea-god, Poseidon. The 'sea monster' whose bones are on display was probably a whale. A walk from the monastery through shady olive groves and along paths first marked out by the Venetians will bring you to the village of Lakones and a bird's-eye view of the dramatic coastline and Paleokastritsa itself - look for the ruins of clifftop Angelokastro Castle (see SIGHTSEEING 3) from which signals were sent to Corfu Town. See BEACHES 2, EXCURSION 2, WALK 3.

Passport and Customs: A visa is not required to enter Corfu but a valid passport is essential for a stay of up to three months (citizens of non-EC member countries may be subject to some restrictions - enquire at travel agents). To extend your length of stay apply to the Aliens Bureau (tel: 39494) or at the Greek Embassy in your home country. No vaccination certificates are required unless travelling from a country with a known epidemic. There are no restrictions on the import of foreign currency, but if you wish to leave with a large sum of money it must have been declared on arrival or you must have documents proving you received the money from outside the country during the course of your stay (apply to a bank for information).

Paxi: The smallest of the main Ionian Islands (10 km by 4 km) with a population of approximately 2250. The island is covered in forests of grapevine and olive trees; many of the latter are extremely old and have grown to an immense size; others have been twisted and bent into extraordinary shapes. Exceptionally clear blue waters will prove irre-

sistible for divers and snorkellers and although beaches are mainly shingle there are plenty of flat rocks for diving and coves for sun-bathing. Gaios, the main town and port, is a pleasant little community with some gracious 19thC houses and a small white church. Boat trips leave from here to various destinations, and bicycles and mopeds can be hired. There is good bathing (shingle beach) at the northern seaside village of Laka which lies in a sheltered bay; notice the unusual low-built houses here, painted in various shades of brown and blue and you may be lucky enough to hear the particularly beautiful Russian bells ring out from the Byzantine church (rung on request). Interesting boat trips around Paxi might include the following: west coast - the splendid Seven Seas caves and the towering Ortholithos rock, the Grotto of Ypapanti (Poseidon's Cave) and the white Mousmouli Cliffs (boat from Laka or on a round-the-island excursion from Gaios) and Mogonissi, a small islet to the south of Gaios, owned by the three brothers who run the restaurant there and operate the boat which leaves every 30 min; it also has a sandy beach and camp site; east coast - Panayia, another small islet with thermal springs and a shrine to the Virgin Mary which attracts pilgrims. On 15 August (Assumption) there is a celebration in the square at Gaios.

Accommodation can be difficult to find on Paxi and, because of the danger of fire, camping outside recognized sites is forbidden. Hotel accommodation is minimal but there are some rooms available in private houses. Try Paxi Beach Bungalows, 3 km south of Gaios, tel: 0662 31211. An overnight stay will allow plenty of time to see Paxi, including a trip to its tiny satellite island, Andipaxi. See **ISLANDS**.

Pets: Small domestic pets may be brought on to the island but are not really welcomed by the Greeks. Certificates declaring that the animal has had a rabies vaccination within the previous 12 months and that the animal is free from disease must be obtained from a vet in the place of origin. SOS Animal Welfare Society, Mrs M. Colla, 17 Dinou Theotoki, tel: 39663.

Police: There are three separate branches: the Tourist Police (Spianada, Corfu Town, tel: 30265) whose officers wear a pale grey uniform and are responsible for visitors' problems such as accommodation or complaints (their counterparts the rural branch are responsible for areas outside Corfu); the Rural Police (Parados Gerassimou Markora, tel: 109) whose officers wear a shoulder belt and white motorcycle helmets; and the Municipal Police (Leoforos Alexandras, tel: 38568) who wear different colours of uniform according to the season and drive white patrol cars. See **Emergencies.**

Post Offices: Central Post Office, Alexandras Av, open 0730-2000. Facilities include a *post restante* service, stamps, and currency exchange. Leave packets and registered letters open as the clerk will want to check the contents. Post boxes are yellow and stamps may also be purchased at the shop where you buy your cards, and at some kiosks.

Public Holidays: 1 Jan. - New Year's Day; 6 Jan. - Epiphany; First Day of Lent; 25 Mar.- Independence Day; Good Friday; Easter Sunday; Easter Monday; 1 May - Labour Day; Whit Monday; 21 May - Enosis Day (Ionian Islands only); 11 Aug. - St Spyridon Procession; 15 Aug. - Assumption of the Virgin Mary; 28 Oct. - Ochi Day; 25 Dec. - Christmas Day; 26 Dec. - St Stephen's Day. See **Events**.

Radio and Television: The national Greek radio stations are as follows: ERT 1st programme (1008 KHz/91.80 MHz) - daily weather forecast and sea conditions in English at 0630 and the news at 0740 in English, French, German and Arabic. ERT2 (981 KHz) - news in English and French at 1420 and 2120. ERT 2nd programme (93.80 MHz) - music, both Greek and foreign. ERT 3rd programme (666 KHz) - classical music.
Two TV channels ERT1 and ERT2 operate from 1730-2400 Mon.-Fri. and 1100-0100 at weekends and occasionally show American, English and German films.

Religious services: *Roman Catholic:* Church in Town Hall Square (opposite the Town Hall). Sunday and holiday Masses as follows: June-Sept. 0730, 0830, 1000, 1900; Oct.-May 0800, 0900, 1000, 1800. Daily 0800. *Jewish Synagogue:* near New Fortress. There is a small Jewish community of two to three hundred. *Anglican:* 21 Mavili St.

Restaurants: Dining alfresco is a major part of Corfu's appeal, particularly to visitors from more northerly climes - choose from tables on terraces and pavements, in courtyards and gardens. Lunch is generally served from 1200 onwards and establishments tend to stay open until very late, usually 0200 or 0300. Diners are welcome to visit the kitchen and to indicate their choice.
The bill will always show two prices: the first is without service and the second, which you pay, is including service. In Corfu Town try the Liston (see SIGHTSEEING 1) for cafés, fast food outlets and restaurants. The Anemomylos area, which is just outside Corfu Town, also offers a wide variety of popular restaurants, tavernas and steak houses. See RESTAURANTS, **Eating out**, **Food**.

Royal Palace: See **Palace of St Michael and St George**.

Smoking: Most international brands of cigarette are available at late-night kiosks all over the island. Greek cigarettes cost from about 70 Drs and foreign brands 150-200 Drs. There is no smoking on buses, in cinemas, theatres and museums, *etc.*

Sports: See **Cricket.**

St Spyridon: St Spyridon was born in Cyprus in the 4thC AD and was a shepherd before first becoming a monk then a bishop. He was renowned for his piety and the performance of some minor miracles. He died in AD 350 and his body was taken to Constantinople but was later to be hurriedly removed, wrapped in a straw basket and tied to the back of a donkey, before the Turks overran the city in the 15thC. He is much loved by the Corfiots who credit him with performing several miracles. See **CHURCHES & MUSEUMS, Church of St Spyridon, Events.**

Taxis: There are two taxi ranks, one at the Old Port and the other on G. Theotoki Street. Others will be found on the Spianada and at San Rocco Square. All taxis have meters - insist that the drivers use them. Radio Taxi - tel: 33811/33812 from anywhere on the island.

Telephones and Telegrams: Calls are made from OTE (Greek Telecommunications Organization) offices . The main office (24-hr

service) is at 3 Mantzarou (behind Central Post Office). Fill in a form and wait for your connection, which can take up to one hour. Cheap rates are after 2100 and at weekends. Telephone boxes (blue for local calls, orange for long-distance calls) accept 10-Dr coins. The code for Corfu Town for outside callers is 0661. International dialling codes from Corfu: UK 0044, USA 001, Republic of Ireland 00353, France 0033, Italy 0039. To obtain a reversed charge call contact the operator by dialling 161 for a call outside Europe or 151 for Europe (facility available Mon.-Fri. only). Dial 162 for an English-speaking operator. Telegrams can be sent from OTE offices or tel: 155.

Time Differences: Corfu is two hours ahead of Britain BST, and two hours ahead of GMT.

Tipping: Service is always included in restaurant and hotel bills although it is also customary to tip the chambermaid or waiter if you are satisfied with the service. Taxi drivers, waiters and hairdressers are normally tipped 10%; chambermaids 50 Drs per week; porters 30 Drs.

Toilets: There are public toilets on San Rocco Square and at the edge of the Esplanade opposite the Olympic Airways office (the attendant will expect a tip of 20 Drs), although visitors are recommended to use the toilets in bars and cafés wherever possible.

Tourist Information: The NTOG (National Tourist Organisation of Greece) office is in the Palace of St Michael and St George, tel: 39730/30520. The service here is very helpful and efficient and you can pick up free maps, schedules, programmes and so on. The assistants speak English, French, Italian and German. The Tourist Police headquarters are also in the Palace, tel: 30265. The *Corfu News* (see **Newspapers**) is a valuable source of information and carries full details of what's on.

Town Hall: A fine example of 17thC Venetian architecture, the building became a theatre in 1720 and now houses the offices of the town's administrators. There is a bust of Doge Francesco Morosini (military

leader who defeated the Turks in the Peloponnese War, 1684-87) on the external east wall. See **SIGHTSEEING 1**.

Yachting: Yachts entering Greek waters for the first time must make themselves known to the Port Authorities, tel: 30481. Corfu Port (Garitsa Bay) has moorings for several dozen yachts and good facilities. In Xen Stratigou (Old Port) there are ships' chandlers and other shops supplying specialist goods such as anchors, compasses, navigation lights as well as maps, books and magazines. Try Force 5 at No. 34, tel: 25051/42815.

Zakinthos: The island is about 27 km by 38 km with a population of approximately 30,000 of whom almost one third live in Zakinthos Town. Strangely reminiscent of England with its country lanes and lush, green fields divided by hedges Zakinthos is one of the least-spoilt and tourist-orientated of the Ionian Islands. Zakinthos Town, the island's capital, was largely reconstructed after the 1953 earthquake and retains its 'old world' atmosphere although few genuine old buildings remain. See the ruins of the Old Fortress on the hill behind the town and the church of Agios Dionysus (3 km towards Argassi beach). The town museum has a collection of icons from the 16th-19thC and some post-Byzantine wall paintings (open 0830-1445 Mon., Wed., Sat., 0800-1300 Sun.). The poets Solomos and Calvos were born in Zakinthos and there is a museum dedicated to them in Agios Moikos Square. The roads on Zakinthos are in fairly good condition and there is a reliable bus service. Macherados (13.5 km on Laganas road) has two 14thC churches, one half-ruined and the other, Agia Mavra, with a splendid interior and a beautiful icon. Enjoy the exceptional views of the island from the scrub-covered plateau at Agios Nicolas (27 km from Zakinthos Town near west coast) and travel further north to Volimes, a large town with a Venetian tower and 12th-14thC frescoes. The magical Blue Caves, where the play of light on the water refracted and reflected a thousand times creates a spellbinding show of colour, are on the north-ernmost tip of the island, accessible by road from Volimes or by boat from St Nicholas Bay. A rather different experience awaits visitors to Xyngia Cave (on the north-east coast) as it shelters a sulphurous spring.

Laganas, on south coast, is the island's only true resort and has a fine sandy beach with unusual rock formations whilst Keri, on the south peninsula, is a sleepy, friendly village at the foot of the hills; the 17thC church here is worth a look and there are some strange pitch springs in the bay. Allow two days to visit the island; there are hotels (try Strada Marina, 16 Lomvardou St., Zakinthos Town, tel: 0695 22761 or Galaxy, Laganas Beach, tel: 0695 72271) and rooms in private houses. Access is by ferry from Killini on Greek mainland (connections with Athens) or by air. See **ISLANDS**.